THE AMAZING WORLD OF GUMBALL Volume One Scholastic Edition, July 2015. Published by KaBOOM!, a division of Boom Entertainment, Inc. THE AMAZING WORLD OF GUMBALL, CARTOON NETWORK, the logos, and all related characters and elements are trademarks of and © Turner Broadcasting System Europe Limited, Cartoon Network. (S15) Originally published in single magazine form as FREE COMIC BOOK DAY 2014 KABOOM! SUMMER BLAST, THE AMAZING WORLD OF GUMBALL No. 1-4. © Turner Broadcasting System Europe Limited, Cartoon Network. (S14) All rights reserved. KaBOOM!™ and the KaBOOM! logo are trademarks of Boom Entertainment, Inc., registered in various countries and categories. All characters, events, and institutions depicted herein are fictional. Any similarity between any of the names, characters, persons, events, and/or institutions in this publication to actual names, characters, and persons, whether living or dead, events, and/or institutions is unintended and purely coincidental. KaBOOM! does not read or accept unsolicited submissions of ideas, stories, or artwork.

For information regarding the CPSIA on this printed material, call: (203) 595-3636 and provide reference RICH# - 619195. A catalog record of this book is available from OCLC and from the KaBOOM! website, www.kaboom-studios.com, on the Librarians Page.

BOOM! Studios, 5670 Wilshire Boulevard, Suite 450, Los Angeles, CA 90036-5679. Printed in USA. First Printing.
ISBN: 978-1-60886-433-1, eISBN: 978-1-61398-287-7

The AMAZING WORLD OF GUMBALL

created by
Ben BOCQUELET

written by
FRANK GIBSON

illustrated by
TYSON HESSE
with PAULINA GANUCKEAU

ads by
YEHUDI MERCADO

"THE AMAZING JOURNAL COMIC OF DARWIN"
written & illustrated by
PRANAS NAUJOKAITIS

cover by
ZACHARY STERLING

designer
JILLIAN CRAB

assistant editors
WHITNEY LEOPARD
& MARY GUMPORT

editor
SHANNON WATTERS

With Special Thanks to
Marisa Marionakis, Rick Blanco, Nicole Rivera, Conrad Montgomery,
Meghan Bradley, Curtis Lelash and the wonderful folks at Cartoon Network.

CHAPTER ONE
COOL

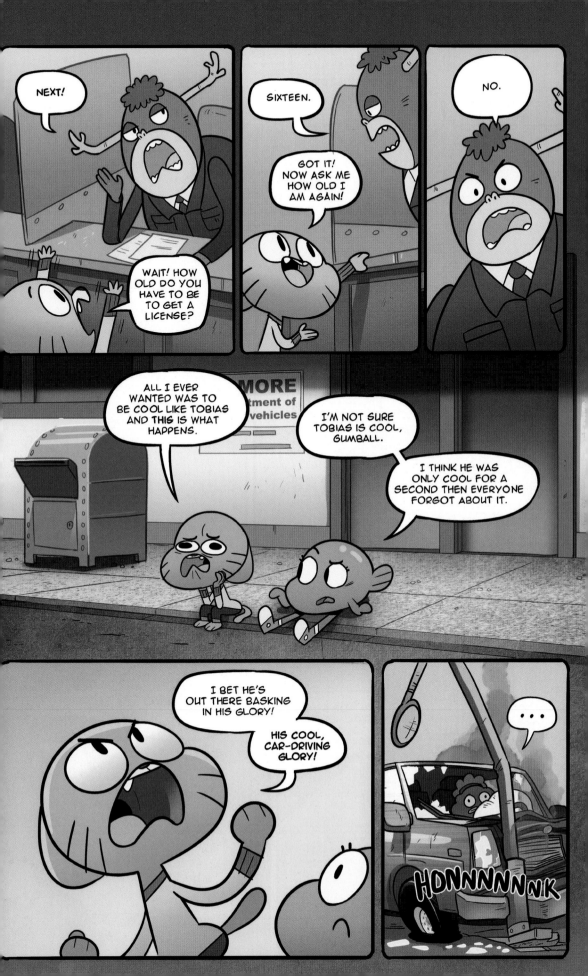

TINA!

DA-DUM

I NEED...

A FAVOR.

A FAVOR?

FROM ME?

PLEEEEASE!

I'LL OWE YOU ONE!

RRING

EXCUSE ME, ELMORE JUNIOR HIGH, IF I MAY HAVE YOUR ATTENTION...

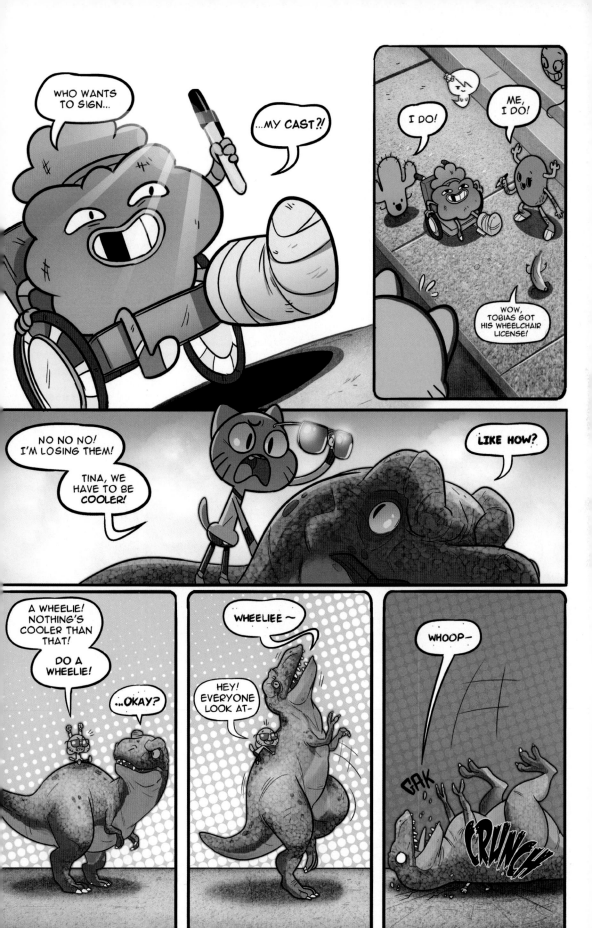

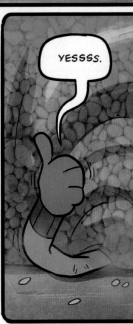

END

CHAPTER TWO
KARATE

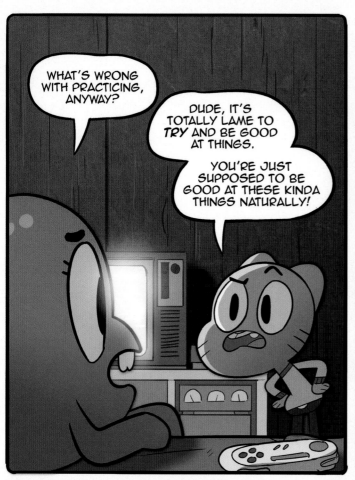

WHAT'S WRONG WITH PRACTICING, ANYWAY?

DUDE, IT'S TOTALLY LAME TO *TRY* AND BE GOOD AT THINGS.

YOU'RE JUST SUPPOSED TO BE GOOD AT THESE KINDA THINGS NATURALLY!

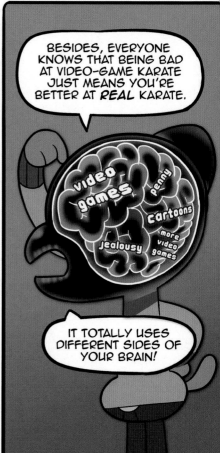

BESIDES, EVERYONE KNOWS THAT BEING BAD AT VIDEO-GAME KARATE JUST MEANS YOU'RE BETTER AT *REAL* KARATE.

video games

penny

cartoons

jealousy

more video games

IT TOTALLY USES DIFFERENT SIDES OF YOUR BRAIN!

WAIT, WHAT DO YOU KNOW ABOUT REAL KARATE?

EVERYTHING, MY DARWIN.

I SUPPOSE YOU'RE OLD ENOUGH NOW TO HEAR THE TRUTH ABOUT MY...

...*DARK PAST.*

WHY DOES EVERYONE IN THIS FAMILY HAVE A DRAMATIC BACK-STORY?

I hate this tree.

LONG AGO, I EFFORTLESSLY BECAME A MASTER OF KARATE.

I hate everything.

I ROAMED THE LAND, HELPING THOSE WHO NEEDED IT THE MOST.

I hate crust.

SADLY, MY POWER GREW TOO GREAT AND IT HURT THE ONES I LOVED.

But I loved sandwich

ON THAT DAY I SWORE TO NEVER KARATE AGAIN.

DO YOU WANNA TEACH ME KARATE?

OKAY.

ALL RIGHT.

BEAT UP THIS CAR.

WHAT?

IF VIDEO GAMES HAVE TAUGHT ME ANYTHING...

...IT'S THAT KARATE MASTERS ARE SO COOL THAT THEY BEAT UP CARS FOR NO REASON.

I'M...NOT SO SURE ABOUT THIS. HOW DO I EVEN BEAT UP A CAR?

I DUNNO, JUMP AROUND AND YELL AND STUFF?

KARATE ISN'T ABOUT *RULES*, DARWIN.

IT'S ABOUT *FEELING*.

I CAN DO THIS.

GO, MY SON.

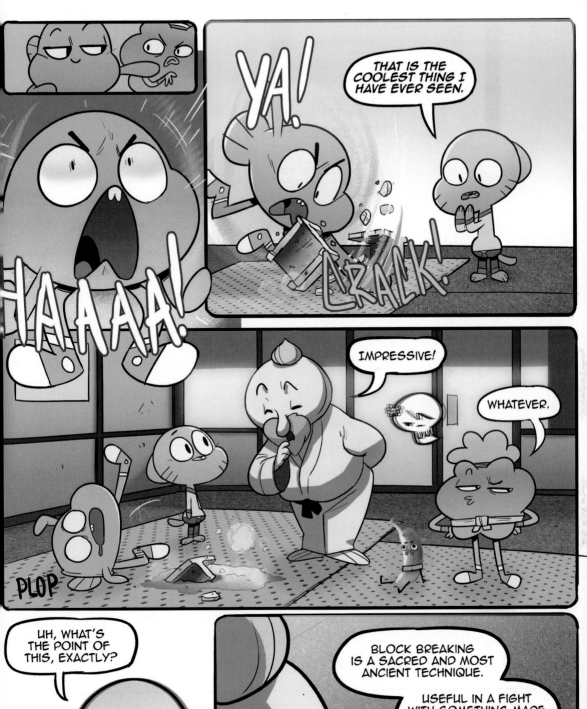

YA!

THAT IS THE COOLEST THING I HAVE EVER SEEN.

HAAAA!

CRACK!

IMPRESSIVE!

WHATEVER.

PLOP

UH, WHAT'S THE POINT OF THIS, EXACTLY?

BLOCK BREAKING IS A SACRED AND MOST ANCIENT TECHNIQUE.

USEFUL IN A FIGHT WITH SOMETHING MADE OF ROCK, SUCH AS A ROCK MONSTER OR UH, A BUILDING.

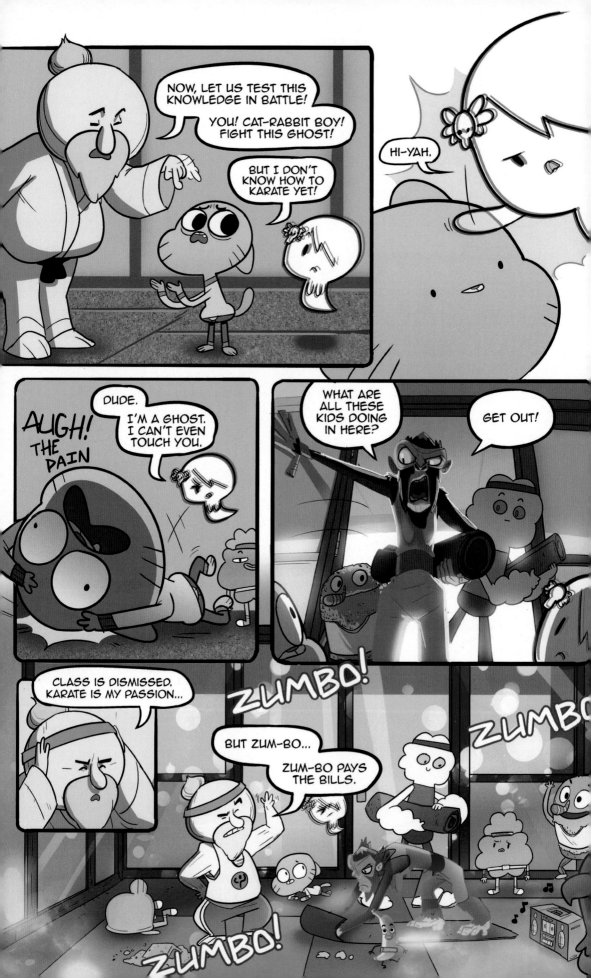

SO BOYS, HOW WAS YOUR FIRST DAY AT KARATE?

WELL...

I'M REALLY BAD AT IT.

AND MY POWER IS SO IMMENSE THAT I DARE NOT LEARN TO EXPRESS IT LEST I ENDANGER MYSELF AND OTHERS!

LET'S QUIT!

OH NO YOU DON'T! I ALREADY PAID FOR TEN LESSONS!

WUB

WUB

WUB

WUB
WUB

WHAT WAS THAT OMINOUS RUMBLING...?

DARWIN, IT'S UP TO YOU! YOU ARE OUR DOJO'S ONLY HOPE TO WIN!

WAIT, WHAT? I'VE ONLY HAD ONE LESSON.

I MUST TELL YOU A SECRET, MY SON.

NO ONE HAS EVER ACTUALLY BROKEN THAT CONCRETE BLOCK IN THE HISTORY OF KARATE.

YOU ARE THE CHOSEN ONE!

WHAT ABOUT ME, HOW AM I SPECIAL?

I WILL PUT YOU OUT FIRST AND HOPEFULLY TOBIAS' FISTS WILL GROW WEARY AFTER HITTING YOU SO MUCH!

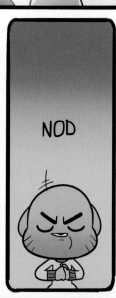

NOD

ROUND ONE

I AM THE DRAGON! I SPREAD MY MIGHTY WINGS AND RO--

PAK!

ALL MY TRAINING HAS LED TO THIS...

...

SCOOT SCOOT

LOW KICK!

LOW KICK!

LOW KICK!

HEY, CUT IT OUT!

POW POW POW

LOW KICK!

LOW KICK!

QUIT USING THE SAME MOVE!

THIS IS THE STUPIDEST FIGHT I'VE EVER SEEN.

WHOOPS

TOBIAS TRIPPED AND FELL, SO HE LOSES!

SO SAYETH THE ANCIENT RULES OF KARATE!

HOORAY.

CHAPTER THREE
TAG:
THE BETRAYAL

SLAM

HEY! WHERE ARE YOU GOING!?

WAIT FOR ME!

WHA--

ELMORE JUNIOR HIGH

REMEMBER YOUR TRAINING, KIDS!

NOT IT

NOT IT

NOT IT FWOOMP!

NOT IT FWOOMP!

NOT IT FWOOMP!

CRASH!

HELLO?

IS ANYBODY HOME?

PSST. OVER HERE.

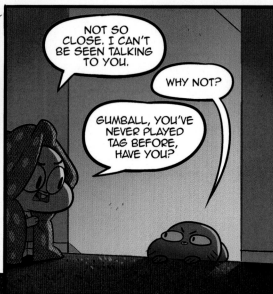

NOT SO CLOSE. I CAN'T BE SEEN TALKING TO YOU.

WHY NOT?

GUMBALL, YOU'VE NEVER PLAYED TAG BEFORE, HAVE YOU?

OF COURSE I HAVE!

ALL THE TIME!

NO, NOT ONCE ACTUALLY.

WELL LET ME FILL YOU IN...

IN THE TOWN OF ELMORE, THE GAME OF TAG IS A DIRE LAST RESORT IN RESOLVING A CONFLICT.

ITS RULES ARE IRON-CLAD. EACH FATEFUL OUTCOME RECORDED UPON THE PAGES OF HISTORY.

IT'S A WAR. AND IT WILL WEAR YOU DOWN UNTIL YOU'D TAG YOUR OWN MOTHER JUST TO FEEL SWEET FREEDOM!

WOW, SIS! THANKS FOR ALL THE INFO! VERY INFORMATIVE!

PUT 'ER THERE!

AND GRIM!

NICE TRY.

YOU'D BETTER TAG SOMEONE ELSE AND FAST. AS WE SPEAK, WORD IS TRAVELLING OUT THROUGH THE EMERGENCY TAG BROADCAST SYSTEM.

GUMBALL IS IT! WE REPEAT: GUMBALL IS IT!

HELLO? HOW DOES THIS WORK?

WHERE DID I GET THIS?!

PING!

MOM! MOM! MOM! MOM!

YES, GUMBALL? WHAT IS IT?

CAN I... GET A HUG?

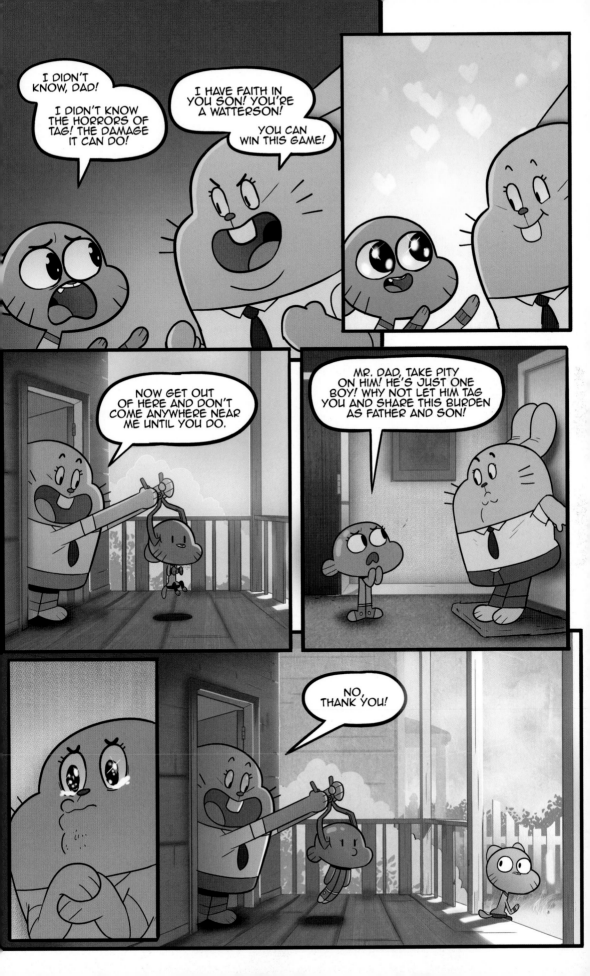

THAT NIGHT
HUFF! HUFF!
HOT FISH
HUFF!
HUFF!
HUFF! HUFF!
I'M
IT
AAAAH!
GUILT

WELL...BOYS, I DON'T KNOW WHAT TO SAY.

I'M TOUCHED!

YES YOU ARE, MISS SIMIAN.

AND YOU'RE ALSO...

"IT"

END

HOT DOG Fighter

6 Players

Online

85 Fighters

Kosher

YEHUDI MERCADO

RELISH THE BATTLE

CHAPTER FOUR
THE BLACK OUT

SPUT
SPUT

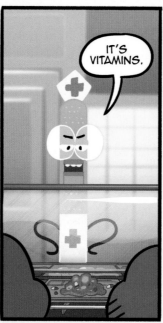

IT'S VITAMINS.

HAIR

...

WASN'T EVEN HUNGRY.

ME EITHER!

GRUMBLE

GRUMBLE

DON'T WORRY, BUDDY.

LET'S JUST GET BACK TO PARTY CLASS AND WE'LL HAVE SO MUCH FUN IT WILL TAKE OUR MINDS OFF OF OUR CRIPPLING HUNGER!

BRRINNG!

WELL...UM...
WELCOME...TO...
YOURRR CLASSSS.

OH GOSH, WHAT IS IT THAT TEACHERS DO, AGAIN?

THEY MAKE ME SAD.

OF COURSE! WELL THEN LET'S HAVE A TEST!

LET'S TAKE ONE HUNDRED TESTS!

TESTS FOR DAYS!

MEANWHILE

PRINCIPAL
ROCKY

I'M THE PRINCIPAL NOW.

I DON'T KNOW WHAT I WAS EXPECTING.

RAINBOW FACTORY COMPLAINTS DEPARTMENT! THIS IS NICOLE!

RAINBOW FACTORY

WAIT, HOW MANY COMPLAINTS? I CAN'T HANDLE ALL OF THOSE TODAY!

NO, I CAN'T STAY FOR AN EXTRA HOUR! I HAVE TO GO HOME TO MY FAMILY!

03:00

YES, I HAVE A HUSBAND!

SIGH

FINE!

CLICK!

GUMBALL'S DOLTOR

MOM

HOME

RING RING

HECK, A LITTLE SNACK COULDN'T HURT US!

NOW LET'S SEE, THERE'S THREE OF US SO WE'LL NEED THREE TIMES AS MUCH FOOD.

AND THREE TIMES ONE IS...

DELICIOUS!

I'LL JUST...

GET ALL THIS...

IN HERE!

NICOLE WILL BE SO PROUD OF ME WHEN SHE GETS--

BEEP

POOMF!

HMM...

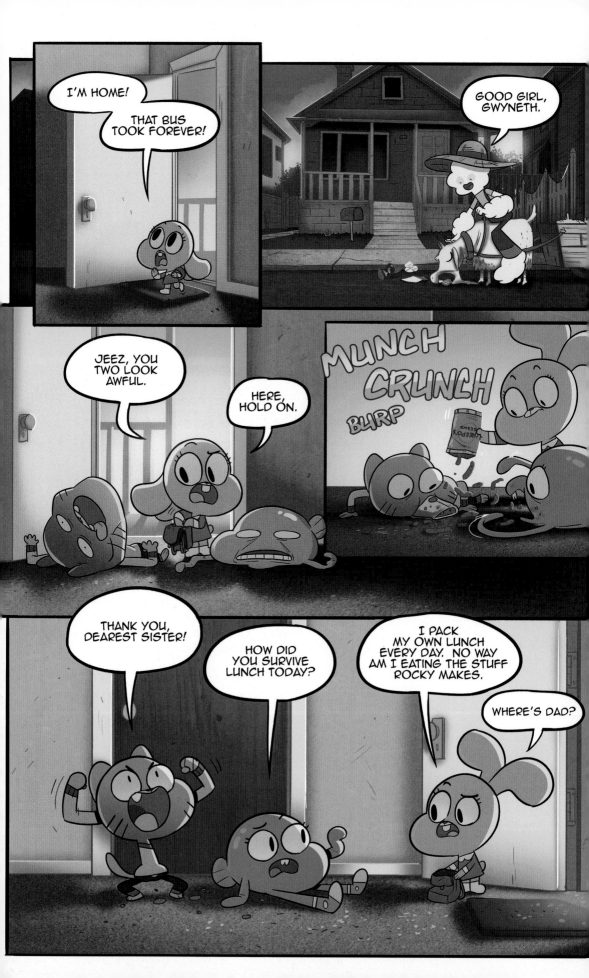

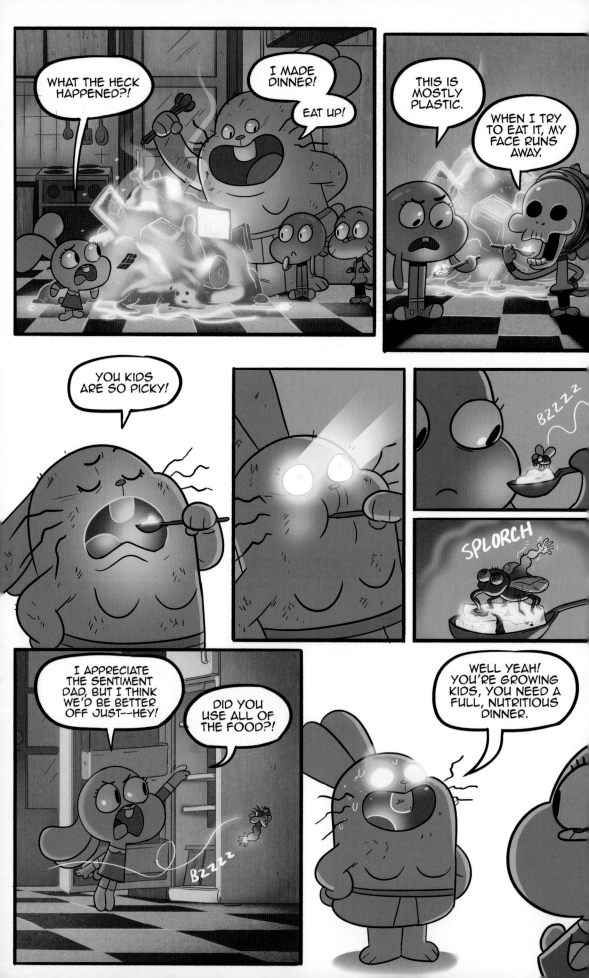

LET'S JUST GO TO THE STORE.

YEAH, I'M STILL HUNGRY!

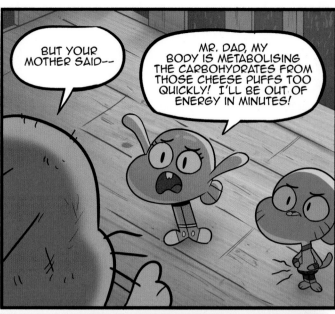

BUT YOUR MOTHER SAID--

MR. DAD, MY BODY IS METABOLISING THE CARBOHYDRATES FROM THOSE CHEESE PUFFS TOO QUICKLY! I'LL BE OUT OF ENERGY IN MINUTES!

I DON'T KNOW WHAT THAT MEANS BUT I'M STILL HUNGRY!

OH JEEZ!

DAD, YOU MUST HAVE KNOCKED THE POWER OUT FOR THE WHOLE TOWN!

OH NO! NICOLE ISN'T GOING TO BE PROUD OF ME AT ALL!

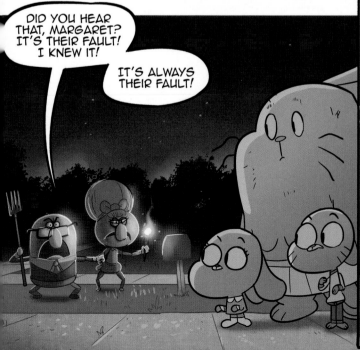

DID YOU HEAR THAT, MARGARET? IT'S THEIR FAULT! I KNEW IT!

IT'S ALWAYS THEIR FAULT!

GET THEM!

QUICK, KIDS! HIDE IN THE CAR!

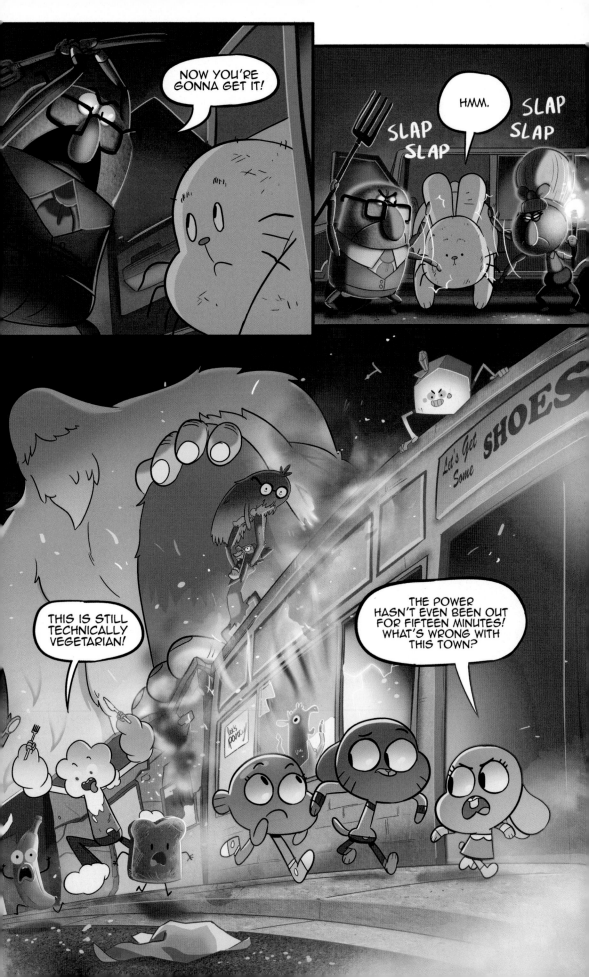

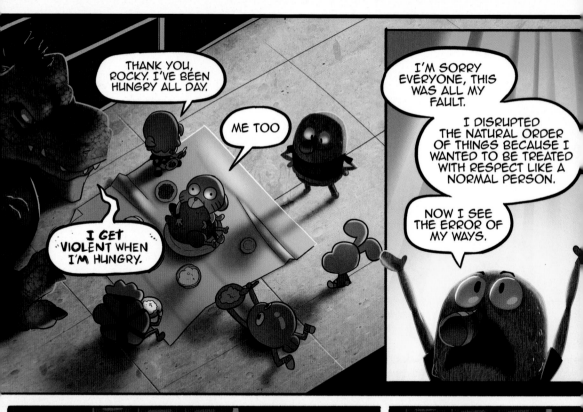

THE END

GUM STORAGE

ASK ABOUT OUR PRE-CHEWED PACKAGE.

```
//Program Dance St
%include <left fo
Using name (Left
Int main ()
[compress]
count five be

cin>> "Heel'
hhm>> "Toe'

total = r
target =
return
//***

Enter music style
1) Rhumba
```

HOW TO DANCE LIKE BOBERT in 6,753 Lines of Code.

4) Disco
5) Western

Forbidden Crush
When Carmen Met Alan

Books of Love

YEHUDI MERCADO

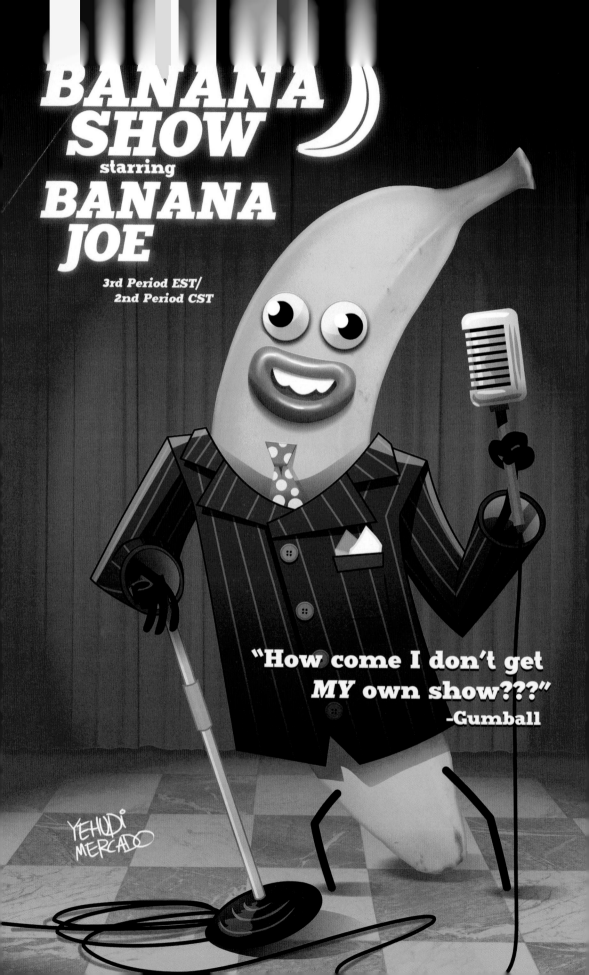

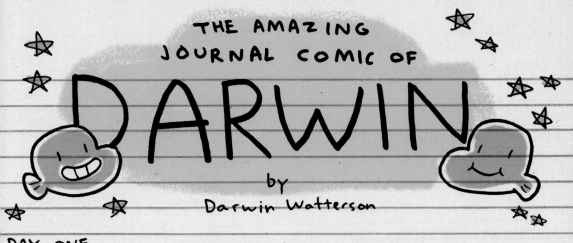

THE AMAZING JOURNAL COMIC OF DARWIN

by
Darwin Watterson

DAY ONE

MISS SIMIAN IS HAVING US KEEP A JOURNAL COMIC FOR A WEEK...

BLAH BLAH BLAH

GUMBALL DOESN'T TAKE IT WELL...

LAME!

TRASH

BUT I WANT TO DO A GREAT JOB AT THIS.

TOO BAD I'M JUST AN ORDINARY FISH BOY WITH A VERY ORDINARY LIFE...

SIGH...

DAY TWO

HOW CAN I HOLD THINGS IF I DON'T HAVE FINGERS?

I'M FREAKING OUT, DUDE!

DAY THREE

GUMBALL AND MRS. MOM
ARE BLUE CATS.

ANAIS AND MR. DAD
ARE PINK RABBITS.

I AM

AN ORANGE FISH.

MAYBE I ATE TOO
MANY CARROTS
GROWING UP...

HMM...

DAY FOUR

OH BOY! LUNCH TIME!

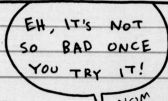

AGGHHHH!
FISH
STICKS!

EH, IT'S NOT
SO BAD ONCE
YOU TRY IT!

NOM
NOM
NOM

HOLY COW!
I'M
DELICIOUS!

Stay in the Nurse's Office All Day!

YUMMY

ViTAMIN
T

PLACEBO FLAVOR

Ø

Endorsed by Teri!

Teri is Not a
Medical Professional

Does Not Cure
Paper Cuts

Tooth Brush
Too Small?

Try NOT
Brushing
Your Teeth!

I'll just chew
Gumball!

YEHUDI
MERCADO

COVER GALLERY

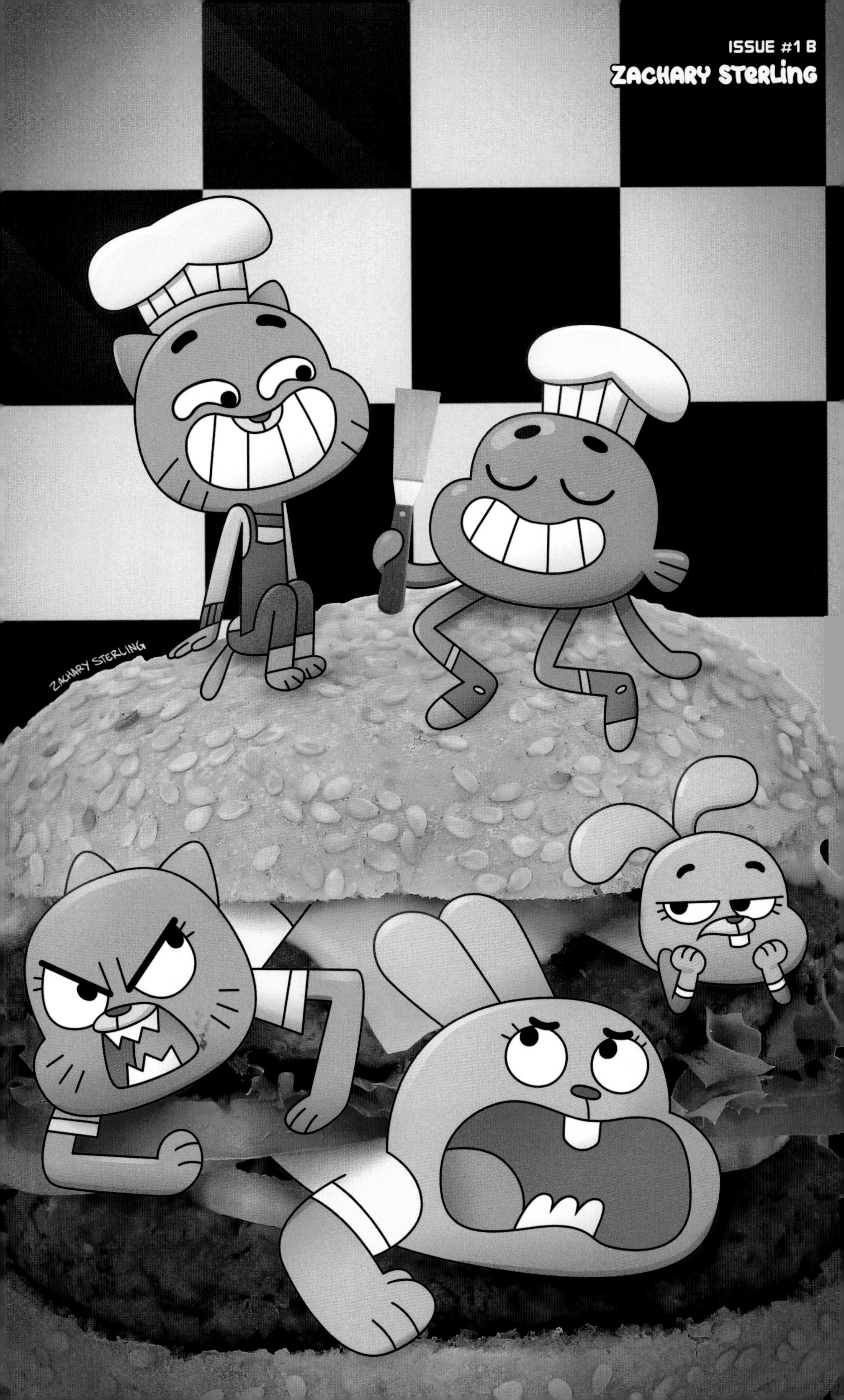

ISSUE #1 C
PAULINA GANUCKEAU

ISSUE #1 DENVER COMIC CON
TYSON HESSE

The
AMAZING
WORLD OF
GUMBALL™

ISSUE #2 A
MISSY PENA

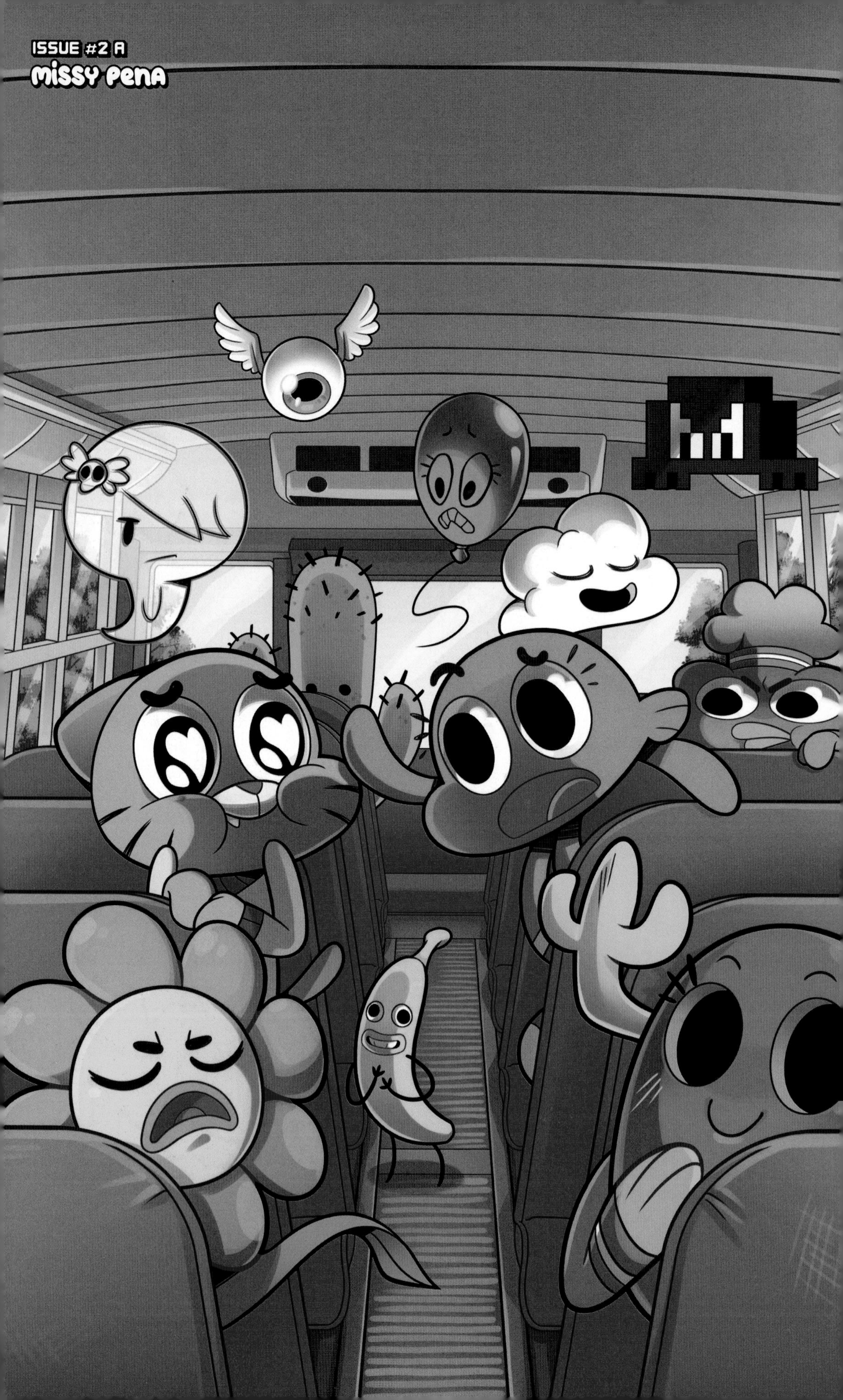

ISSUE #2 C
Aimee Fleck

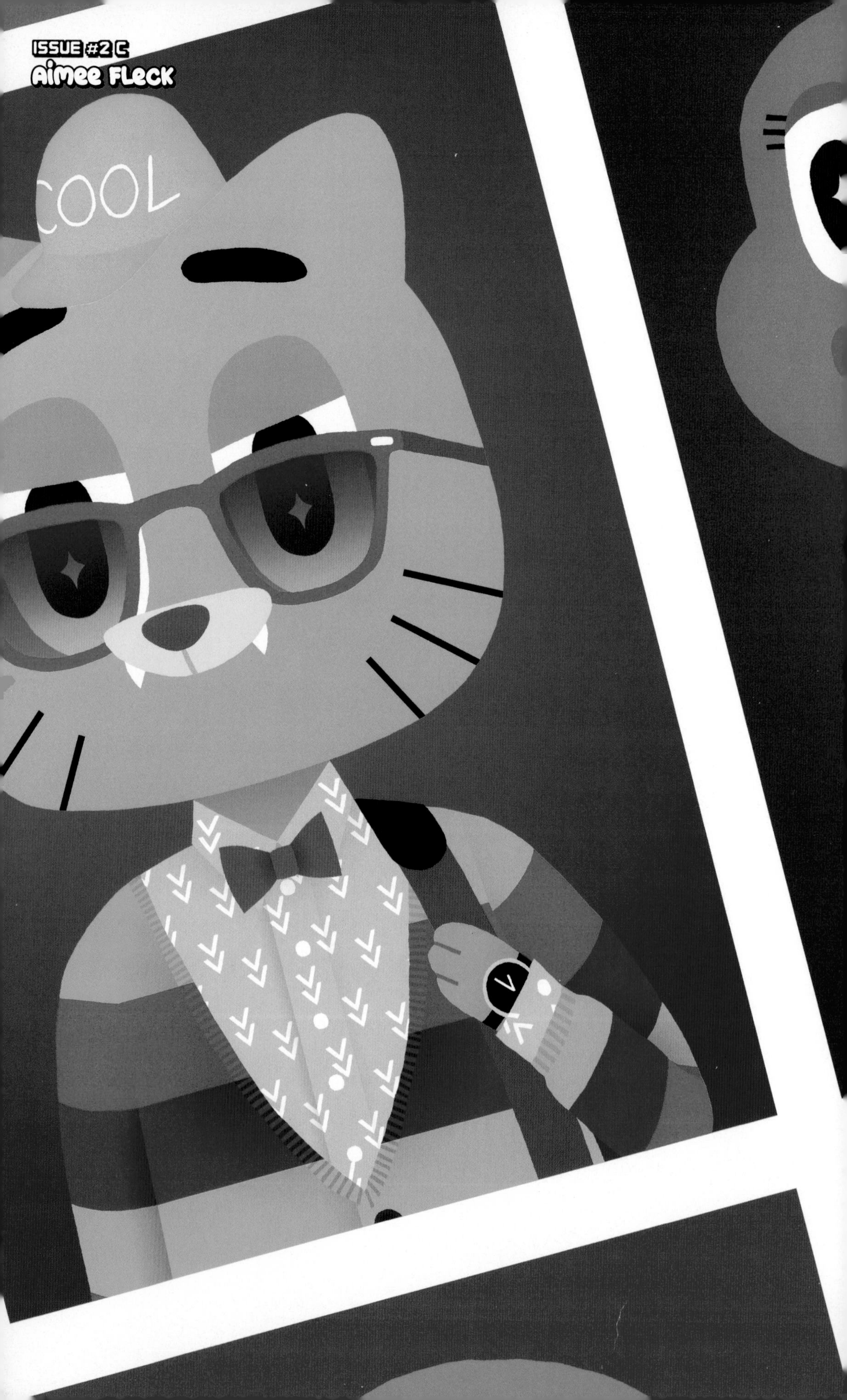

ISSUE #4 C
JUSTIN OAKSFORD